Viking
raiders and
settlers

A Viking longship.

Inside a Viking
town house.

Many interpretations

This book describes some of the things that happened a long time ago. Very little remains of these times and so much of what is said has, of necessity, to be interpretive. In this book the author has tried to present the generally accepted view of historians.

⚠ Look after our heritage!

It is easy to talk about looking after the environment, but we each have to help. Help is often small things, like being careful when you walk around old buildings, and not leaving scratch marks on anything that you visit. It doesn't take a lot of effort – just attitude.

◄ Viking gravestone.

Curriculum Visions

Curriculum Visions is a registered trademark of Atlantic Europe Publishing Company Ltd.

There's more on-line

There's more about other great Curriculum Visions packs and a wealth of supporting information available at our dedicated web site. Visit:

www.CurriculumVisions.com

◆ *Atlantic Europe Publishing*

First published in 2005 by
Atlantic Europe Publishing Company Ltd.
Copyright © 2005
Atlantic Europe Publishing Company Ltd.

Author
Brian Knapp, BSc, PhD

Editor
Robert Anderson, BA, PGCE

Art Director
Duncan McCrae, BSc

Designed and produced by
EARTHSCAPE EDITIONS

Senior Designer
Adele Humphries, BA, PGCE

Printed in China by
WKT Company Ltd

Viking raiders and settlers – *Curriculum Visions*
A CIP record for this book is available from the British Library

Paperback ISBN 1 86214 423 0
Hardback ISBN 1 86214 425 7

Illustrations (c=centre t=top b=bottom l=left r=right)
Mark Stacey cover illustrations, pages 1, 10–11, 12–13, 15, 16–17, 18–19, 20–21, 22–23, 24, 26, 28–29, 30–31, 33, 35tr, 41; *David Woodroffe* pages 7, 8t, 34–35, 37, 40.

Picture credits
All photographs are from the Earthscape Editions photolibrary except the following: (c=centre t=top b=bottom l=left r=right)
© *The Trustees of The British Museum* page 43; *Shetland Museum* pages 2tl, 3tr, 4t, 8b, 38t, 38b, 39t, 39b; *York Archaeological Trust* cover photograph, pages 2bl, 3b, 4b, 5, 20t, 25t, 25b, 27, 42, 45.

Acknowledgements
The publishers would like to thank the following for their kind help and advice: *British Museum, Shetland Museum* and *York Archaeological Trust.*

This product is manufactured from sustainable managed forests. For every tree cut down at least one more is planted.

Contents

▶ A Viking brooch.

▼ A selection of Viking coins found at York.

Words, names and places

Words in **CAPITALS** are further explained under 'Words, places and names' on pages 46–47.

The Vikings

This book is about VIKINGS – a people who lived just over a thousand years ago. Their first homelands lay in SCANDINAVIA, but they also INVADED and settled in Britain.

The Viking Age in Britain began about 1,200 years ago in the 8th century AD and lasted for 300 years. In England it ended in 1066, but it lasted for centuries longer in Scotland.

Although Viking invasions stopped over a thousand years ago, many words we use today come down to us from the Viking language and many places have names given to them in Viking times.

▶ **A Viking carving of a LONGSHIP. Vikings used longships to trade and make war.**

Quite a few of us even have Viking genes in our blood.

On this page you will learn briefly what happened during Viking times. You'll learn much more as you read through the book.

▼ **The Vikings were skilled blacksmiths as these iron working tools show.**

▼ Viking wooden bowls and spoons.

1 The Vikings lived in Denmark, Norway and Sweden, countries on the other side of the North Sea – to the east of the British Isles.

2 The Vikings were farmers and fishermen who became traders and **WARRIORS**.

3 Some Vikings made hit and run **RAIDS** on the British Isles for about 50 years. Then they began to stay.

4 The places the Norwegian Vikings stayed were in the islands of northern Scotland, and the east coast of Ireland.

5 The Danish Vikings at first landed in small groups. But in the 9th century, they invaded eastern England, sending over thousands of men as a **GREAT ARMY**.

6 The Vikings had to fight the English, the Scots and the Irish. Everywhere they met resistance, but in general their invasions were successful. The most famous **ANGLO-SAXON** king to fight the Vikings was **KING ALFRED**, and he only just managed to stop them from taking over the whole of England.

7 Struggles continued for two hundred years. Sometimes the Anglo-Saxon kings held control, sometimes the Vikings.

8 Even though there were many wars, during this time many Vikings settled down, leaving a legacy of Viking names where they lived.

The Viking homelands

The Viking homelands were in the countries of Scandinavia.

▼ ① The Norwegian Vikings lived in a land of snowy mountains and rocky soils like this. It was a difficult place to live.

The Vikings came from the part of Europe now called **SCANDINAVIA**. The Scandinavian countries are Denmark, Finland, Sweden and Norway (picture ①).

This is where the Vikings began, but the Vikings did not all remain in these countries.

The Viking lands

Scandinavia is in the north of Europe and has long, cold, snowy winters and cool summers.

No part of Scandinavia is easy to farm, and none has supplies of gold, iron or other metals. As a result, the Vikings had to seek the food and other goods they needed from overseas – either by trade or by war. They did both.

The spread of the Vikings

Because the Viking lands were close to the sea, all Vikings were good at fishing, boat-building and sea travel.

Some Vikings traded as far as the Mediterranean Sea, a voyage that would take many months.

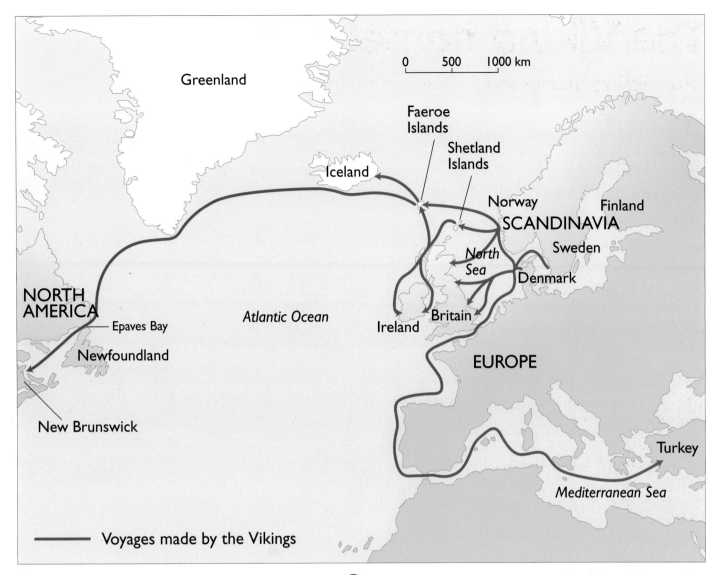

Greenland

0   500   1000 km

Faeroe
Islands

Shetland
Islands

Iceland

Norway   Finland
SCANDINAVIA

North   Sweden
Sea
Denmark

NORTH
AMERICA
— Epaves Bay   Atlantic Ocean   Ireland   Britain

Newfoundland   EUROPE

New Brunswick

Turkey

Mediterranean Sea

——— Voyages made by the Vikings

▲ ② The Vikings traded as far as Turkey. They explored
as far as North America, and they raided and settled in
Britain, Ireland and other neighbouring countries.

As the numbers of Vikings increased, so they began to use up all of the land they could farm. Starting in the 8th century, some Vikings changed from just trading goods to trying to capture goods and new land (picture ②).

For the next three hundred years, the Vikings became some of the most feared warriors in Europe.

Most Vikings chose the shortest sea route they could find. That is why, when the Norwegian Vikings started to raid, they made for Scotland and Ireland.

It might take just two days' sailing to get from Norway to the Shetland Islands. Similarly, Danish Vikings invaded England because it was only a short sea journey away from Denmark.

Who knows...

how the Vikings got their name?

▶ Possibly because they lived in small bays, or viks.

▶ Perhaps from an old Viking word *vikingr* meaning 'pirate' or 'sea-raider'.

Viking writing and names

The Vikings used a writing system very different from the one we use today. They also called themselves after animals and gods.

The Vikings were not great writers. This is one reason we know so little about them. In fact, much of our knowledge of the Vikings comes from books written by the **ANGLO-SAXONS** or by people who wrote about them in later centuries.

Instead of writing things down, the Vikings usually passed important facts from **GENERATION** to generation using oral (spoken) stories.

Vikings called these stories **SAGAS** (see page 14).

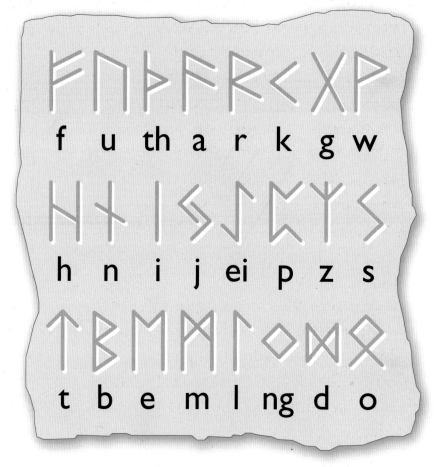

f u th a r k g w

h n i j ei p z s

t b e m l ng d o

▲ ② The original futhark had 24 letters. The modern English alphabet has 26 letters. Notice which of the modern letters were grouped up or missing.

▼ ① This stone from Eshaness in the Shetland Islands shows runic writing.

From time to time, however, they did use a special kind of writing that was made up almost entirely of straight lines. This was because they wrote on stone or bone, not paper, carving or scratching the letters with a blade.

The letters of the Viking alphabet are called **RUNES**. A stone tablet with runes on it is called a runestone (picture ①).

The Viking alphabet changed over the years. At first it had 24 letters, but eventually some were combined and the alphabet became 16 letters. The first letters of the alphabet sounded like f, u, th, a, r and k, and so the alphabet is called the **FUTHARK** (picture ②).

Viking words today

The Vikings conquered parts of Britain, and so many Viking words became part of the shared language of Britain. In this way the language became richer.

We still use many Viking words today. For example, many of the days of the week are named after Viking gods and goddesses (picture ③).

Most words beginning with sc or sk are Viking, for example sky and scatter. Other common words of Viking origin are knife and window.

Names of people

Viking men wanted to appear brave and so named themselves after fierce animals or gods. The Viking name Bjorn, for example, means 'bear'. Modern English names for men that have Viking connections include Eric, Harold and Rolf. And for women they include Ingrid and Thora.

The end of runes

When the Vikings arrived in the British Isles they were **PAGANS** (see page 12). They invaded as fierce warriors with no time or liking for writing. But later generations settled down and became Christian. Those with the most learning (usually monks) also began to write using the alphabet we use today. As a result, the use of runes faded away.

Who knows...

why we know so little about Vikings?

▶ Very few Vikings could read or write, so they wrote down very little about themselves.
▶ They mainly wrote on stone, which is slow and hard work.
▶ The people who lived at the same time as the Vikings were their enemies and so they wrote only about the Vikings' bad side.
▶ Most history written by Vikings was in the form of stories written in Iceland hundreds of years after the events.
▶ Viking houses were usually made of wood and have rotted away.

Tuesday	Wednesday	Thursday	Friday
Tyr's day	Woden's (Odin's) day	Thor's day	Frigg's day

◀ ③ The days of the week named after Viking gods and goddesses.

Kings, chieftains and clans

Vikings organised themselves into kingdoms. Below the kings were many classes of people, including slaves.

You can only hold on to land if you are strong enough to defend it. This is why, from ancient times, people have formed groups for protection.

Groups of people who live together and marry amongst each other are often called CLANS. Clans were ruled by CHIEFTAINS.

Justice by violence

Families and clans worked with rough-and-ready justice. For example, many Viking clans got caught up in violent disputes known as blood-feuds.

An argument might end in a fight. If someone was killed, the dead man's family saw it as their right to take revenge. Blood-feuds sometimes ended by one side paying 'blood-money' as compensation.

Kingdoms

Over time, feuds between clans meant that the most powerful clan took power from the others and increased the size of land over which they ruled. This larger territory became a kingdom.

▼ Viking society was made up of several classes of people.

King

Nobleman (jarl)

Chieftain (landsman)

Warrior/farmer (bondi)

But even a king must defend his land. In Viking times the Danish, Swedish and Norwegian kingdoms often fought with each other. They also fought with their other neighbours – including the British.

Making decisions, passing laws

A kingdom is too big for one person to rule alone. Many decisions have to be taken by other people whom the king knows he can trust. In Viking kingdoms the people given parts of the kingdom to look after were called JARLS (earls). These people were second only to the king in power.

Some jarls were warriors (professional soldiers). They protected the king. Their payment was a share of the BOOTY captured during a raid. There were also young part time fighters called BONDI. Because of this

system it was in everyone's interests to raid on others. Many jarls wanted more power and plotted to overthrow their neighbours and even the king.

Most people were not fighters, however. They were freemen (KARLS) and they worked the land, made goods or were fishermen. But they were not powerless. They formed a kind of parliament called a 'THING', which met to make laws and to decide punishments for criminals.

Slaves

In Viking times, as for centuries before and after, it was common to have slaves, or THRALLS. Slaves were people who had been captured in battle – often former soldiers, but also women and children from captured villages.

They were the lowest people, and the rest of a clan depended on them to work the land and do other heavy jobs while they were away fighting.

Freeman (karl)

Slave (thrall)

Who knows...

who were the most famous Viking kings?

▶ King Sweyn Forkbeard was the first Viking king of England. He ruled from 1013 to 1014.
▶ King Canute the Great (the son of Sweyn) ruled England and Denmark from 1016 to 1035. His two unpopular sons ruled until their deaths in 1040 and 1042.
▶ Harald Hadrade was a king of Norway. He also claimed the throne of England. He attacked England in July 1066 and was killed by the Anglo-Saxon King Harold.
▶ William the Conqueror ended the Anglo-Saxon age in England at the Battle of Hastings in October 1066. He was born in Normandy, France, but was descended from Vikings.

Pagan gods and burials

Vikings were originally pagans. They worshipped many gods and believed that if they died in battle they went to live in a splendid palace called Valhalla.

The Vikings were keen to make sense of the world around them. They wondered who had put them on the Earth. The early Vikings were **PAGANS**. They believed there were a number of gods, who were similar to humans but with great powers.

Viking gods

Vikings worshipped gods whom they called the **AESIR**. The main Viking gods were **ODIN**, **THOR** and **FREY**.

The most important god was Odin (also known as Woden). He was the god of war and also of wisdom. Odin lived in a great hall called **VALHALLA**.

It was the aim of all Viking warriors to join Odin. However, for that to happen they had to die in battle. This explains why Vikings were such ferocious warriors.

Thor was a very strong but less clever god. Thor did battle with giants and monsters, killing them with his hammer. Many Vikings wore a small version of Thor's hammer as a good luck charm.

Frey was the god of life and helped bring in a good harvest. Frey had a sister called Freyja, who was the goddess of birth and love. The wife of Odin was Frigg.

Tyr was the god of justice. Loki was part god and part devil. He could change shape and cause mischief.

▲ ① A king might be buried in one of their ships. It might be floated out to sea or buried under a mound of earth.

Ordinary people would be buried more simply. Instead of a real ship, an outline of a ship made of stones might be put around the grave, much the same as gravestones are used today (see background).

Who knows...

what the Vikings believed in?

The Vikings believed:
▶ men could only go to heaven (Valhalla) if they died in battle, so many were happy to fight to the death.
▶ that the Earth was flat.
▶ that four dwarves (north, south, east and west) held up the sky.
▶ that the first people were born from the sweat of a giant's armpit.
▶ that gods were like super-humans.

Vikings believed that it was important to offer sacrifices to these gods, and for this they held three major festivals each year.

Viking burials

For their journey to the afterlife Vikings believed they would need their possessions from their present life.

As a result, Vikings were buried with precious goods, sometimes even including the ship they owned (picture ①).

In a few cases their slaves and wives were killed and put in the grave with them so that they would have company and slaves in the afterworld.

A 'Viking' saga

Viking boys had to become warriors as soon as they were able. But to become a warrior needed a test of courage. The story, or saga, below tells of Bjorn.

SAGAS were stories made up after the great days of Viking history as a way of remembering the past. Here is the kind of story the Vikings might have told.

Bjorn becomes a warrior

Bjorn was feeling proud. Today, on his 15th birthday, he would go through a test and, if he passed it, he would no longer be a boy, but would become a man.

For years he had watched the men go out and raid as proud warriors, and he would hear them laugh and joke about their deeds and the BOOTY they had brought back. And for years he had envied them.

Now was his chance to prove that he was worthy of joining them in their raids. He would also be allowed to defend the village against attack from neighbouring tribes.

Bjorn looked at his spear. It was long, sturdy and gleaming. He looked at his shield. It was made of stout wood, fashioned into a disc and brightly painted. His gear was surprisingly heavy, and he wondered, just for a second, if he would be able to carry it all.

Suddenly he was summoned in front of the people gathered in the LONGHOUSE. By the fire, seated on a wooden chair, was the chieftain. The chieftain would challenge him to do a deed to prove he had become a man. If he failed he would be disgraced and be as lowly as the slaves that had been captured in battle.

The challenge had been set: he must go alone into the forests, seek a reindeer and bring it back.

Outside it was bitterly cold with snow thick on the ground. Bjorn thought of his name – it meant 'the bear' – and wondered if he would meet a bear in the forest. Swiftly now, he began to search for hoofprints in the snow.

In the longhouse everyone waited, busying themselves about their jobs, but always wondering what was happening to Bjorn on his lonely quest.

The hours passed and then, out of the darkness, Bjorn returned. He was pulling something behind him. The antlers told everyone that it was a fully grown reindeer.

Bjorn came to the fire. Everyone gathered round as he began to tell of how he had tracked and then caught the biggest reindeer in the world…

(Note: this is a modern story; Viking sagas were too long to fit on this page.)

Who knows...

what sagas were?

▶ Sagas were a good way of passing on the history of the people.
▶ They were often tall tales, like fairy tales, made for entertainment.
▶ They were often violent.
▶ They were mainly written centuries after real events.
▶ They were long to while away the long winter nights.

Weblink: www.CurriculumVisions.com

Village life

Many Vikings lived in villages by the shores of rivers or FJORDS.

Vikings were peoples of the land and sea. They did not have the urge to live in towns or cities like the **ROMANS**.

Many people lived in small villages by a river or the sea (picture ①). This was because using boats was the easiest way to get about – the land was mostly forested or marshy and there were few good tracks.

The village

A Viking village would have been a simple collection of scattered homes, each in its own yard. The yard would be fenced off, and there vegetables were grown and small animals – chickens and pigs – were kept.

Earth wall

Harbour and quay

Workshop

The village would also have included some workshops for people who were skilled at crafts, such as carpentry or shipbuilding. In later times, there might also have been a small church.

The village would have been protected from wild animals and attacks by raiders with an earth wall topped with pointed stakes.

The harbour

The most important part of the village was the harbour. This might simply be a riverside beach, or it might have a wooden quay.

Boats arrived in the harbour carrying food or other goods that were needed. At other times they might be carrying just a **BALLAST** of stones after taking goods to a distant port. On arrival, these stones were tipped over the side. Today **ARCHAEOLOGISTS** use the presence of these stones to tell where harbours were once built.

◀ ① A village was a place where people lived, traded and worked. They also kept animals and grew their own vegetables. In wet weather the ground would become very muddy, so timber roadways were laid.

Wooden roadway

Yard

Weblink: www.CurriculumVisions.com

A Viking farm and longhouse

Out in the countryside, the Vikings spent the short Scandinavian summer farming. Here they lived in buildings called longhouses.

In the countryside, Vikings lived in small scattered farms. These were home to one or two karl and bondi families and their slaves (picture ①). In Scandinavia, good farmland was scarce and was usually owned by the local jarl, or nobleman.

Everyone in the settlement had to work the land. The karls and bondi would get part of the harvest for their trouble, but slaves would simply get their food.

▼ ① In the busy summer months, the Viking farmers would gather hay as well as plough the land. The hay was dried on racks and stored for the animals to feed on in winter. It was also the time for other jobs, such as thatching or mending fences.

The longhouse

Everyone, including the animals, lived together in a **LONGHOUSE**. There might also be a **BREWERY**, a **FORGE** and barns to store cereals, salted fish and hay.

Harvests were not always good. In some years there was not enough food, and people could starve to death. It was because Vikings were so worried that there would not be enough food that they became traders and, later on, warriors.

Who knows...

what longhouses were made from?

► In areas with plentiful forest, like Scandinavia, the walls were often made from planks or WATTLE AND DAUB.
► In areas without trees, such as Shetland, the walls were made from stone.
► The roof might be reed thatch or turf or peat blocks.

Town life

Few Vikings lived in towns, but when they did, their surroundings became quite squalid.

The Vikings were not fine builders in stone. They were not even good potters. In Scandinavia they carved their cooking pots and bowls out of a soft rock called soapstone.

▲ ② Some of the many iron implements made by a Viking smith.

▼ ① Towns were places of work and trade, with homes often doubling as workshops.

Each home had a fenced tiny yard at the back and many were cramped together.

Only towards the end of Viking times – when many more Vikings settled in towns and villages and became Christian – did they start to make stone buildings such as churches and learn pottery skills.

Cramped towns

There were few Viking towns. Places like **JORVIK** (York) in Yorkshire and Dyfflin (Dublin) in Ireland are exceptions. Towns (picture ①)

were places of trade and of making things such as iron tools and weapons (picture ②).

Town houses were built close together and were separated only by small yards or alleyways.

Smelly towns

The Vikings had no proper toilets. Neither was there any one to collect the rubbish and carry it away. In the country this didn't matter so much, but in a town the smell of human waste and rotting rubbish must have been around all the time.

Great mounds of waste often built up. We call them **MIDDENS**. The middens were places where people dumped their old rubbish. Sometimes more precious things like jewellery ended up in middens by accident. For this reason, middens are a treasure trove for archaeologists, and it is in old middens that we find many clues to the Viking way of life.

Work and trade

Even chieftains lived in single-roomed wooden houses with **WATTLE AND DAUB** walls and thatched roofs. The roof timbers (gables), however, would have been specially carved.

Many homes would have been part workshop, part living space. Making things simply added to the smell. Tanning leather, blacksmithing, and dyeing cloth were all hot, smelly jobs. Fish drying, too, was a smelly thing to do.

Inside the town house

Viking town homes were a single room in which work, rest and play all happened.

For centuries, Vikings lived together with one or more families sharing a single-roomed house (picture ①). In the countryside, the houses would be bigger and were called longhouses. In the **LONGHOUSES** the home would be shared with the farm animals as well.

Houses were often built with low stone walls. Some houses were even partly underground, so that you stepped down into the house. This meant that houses were less exposed to the weather and so kept them warmer in winter.

The house was made up of a wooden frame built of poles and beams. Sticks were woven across the beams of the roof and thatch (or turf) placed on them to make the house warm and waterproof. A hole was left for smoke to escape.

▼ ① A town house belonging to a prosperous Viking family.

Food and personal belongings hung on the wall and ceiling

Reed and thatch roof

Special seat or high chair for the head of the house or chieftain

Reeds and herbs cover the floor

Chest for keeping valuables

Open hearth

The walls were filled in with planks or with **WATTLE AND DAUB**.

Furniture

Most people sat and slept on earthen or wooden benches placed around the edge of the house. They used furs or fleeces as blankets. Only the houses of the very rich would have had chairs and tables.

Platforms for sleeping and sitting

Loom for weaving

Oak planks. Wattle and daub was also used.

Each family had its own private chest in which it kept its valuables.

Cooking and weaving

Soups and porridges were cooked in a pot hung over the open fire. Meat and fish were roasted.

Food for the winter would be stored in jars and baskets. A little corn would be ground in a **QUERN** each time bread was to be made. Buckets for carrying water were made from wood and strapped around with metal hoops.

Many people made their own woollen clothes (see page 24). They **WOVE** the wool using a loom kept in the corner of the house.

A short life

Viking lives were short. Part of the reason for this is that people got worn out with hard work. Also they did not understand how to prevent disease. Rats and other animals could easily spread plague and other diseases. No one washed their hands after going to the toilet or before handling food.

Who knows...

what it was like to live in a Viking house?

▶ It was always smoky because the fire had no chimney. There was just a hole in the roof.
▶ The fire was always burning because there were no windows and the fire was needed to see by, keep warm and cook on.
▶ There was no privacy. Everyone slept together on wooden benches around the walls. You only got to be alone when you went to the hut used as a toilet.
▶ Vikings had no toilet paper so they used grass or tree leaves.

Viking clothes

Clothes needed to be warm and waterproof as well as long-lasting. Designs for all but the rich were very simple.

After food, clothing was the most important item for a Viking family. Most people wore clothes made of wool (picture ①).

Vikings used the fleece (coat) of sheep. The fleece fell out naturally and could be picked off the ground. Women would then spend long winter nights around fires SPINNING the wool. The wool could then be knitted or WOVEN.

Clothes were DYED red, green, brown, yellow or blue using the juices from plants.

They also made linen, a cloth that used fibres from the FLAX plant.

▼ ① **Clothing of a karl and his family.**

Viking fabrics were often made of tightly twisted (worsted) wool. They also used, linen, horsehair and even dog hair.

People preferred strongly coloured clothes. Birch leaves were used as a yellow dye. Red came from the roots of a plant called northern bedstraw. Blue came from the woad plant, and green from juniper berries.

A typical dress required 30 kilometres of woollen thread.

Everybody – men and women – loved to wear jewellery: rings, bracelets, necklaces and brooches.

Most people wore several layers of clothing to keep warm.

The basic clothes were a shirt (tunic) and trousers. They were fastened with pins and brooches.

Women's and girls' clothes

Women wore a long linen dress. To keep out the cold they wore a woollen tunic over the dress. It was held on to the dress with brooches.

To keep even warmer they wore a woollen shawl. In the winter they wore a woollen cloak and a woollen hat as well. The cloak was fastened with a brooch over the shoulder. Women also wore long woollen stockings and flat leather shoes (picture ②).

▲ ③ A collection of stone beads that would have been threaded together to make a necklace.

Men's and boys' clothes

Viking men wore a long woollen shirt and trousers. A woollen or leather coat called a jerkin went on top of this. They also wore cloaks in cold weather, fastened over the shoulder with a brooch and woollen socks and flat leather shoes or boots.

Warriors also needed a battle dress. This was made of a thick leather coat and a leather helmet. The rich wore an iron helmet and possibly some CHAIN MAIL, although the weight of this made fighting quite difficult.

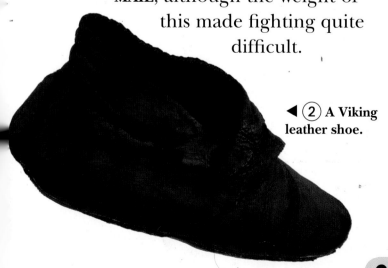

◄ ② A Viking leather shoe.

Make-up and jewellery

Both men and women wore make-up. They also wore jewellery (picture ③), in part to look attractive, but also because they used it as a form of money. Silver armbands, for example, would be removed and a piece cut off to pay for goods. Coins were not common in Viking times.

Did the Vikings...

look and smell good?

▶ In an age where most people in the world did not bathe at all, the Vikings bathed once a week – on a Saturday.

▶ For the rest of the week their clothes probably stank of smoke from the fire in the longhouse.

▶ People expected to live only to their 30s, and looked old very quickly. Both men and women wore make-up to cover up signs of wear and tear.

▶ Viking clothes were very plain so they used dyes and added jewellery to make them stylish.

Viking meals and drink

The Vikings ate basic foods made from what they could grow, rear or catch.

Vikings could not visit a supermarket for food – it all had to be grown, reared or caught locally (picture ①).

Food supplies

Pigs and sheep, chickens and geese were all reared. Hares, deer and wildfowl were caught in the woods. Fish was caught from the rivers and seas (picture ②). Vegetables including onions, carrots and cabbages were grown in small fields or in the yards next to houses.

In the late summer, the woods provided a variety of berries, nuts and fruit.

Preserving food

Meat and fish would quickly go bad if they were not **PRESERVED**. First they were dried on racks, then smoked over the fire or packed with salt.

Fruit was also dried or made into jam using honey.

▼ ① Most meals were a form of soup. From time to time, however, there was a meal of fish or game.

▲ ② Fishing hooks and weights.

If there was a poor harvest then the amount of food that could be stored would be too small to stretch to the next harvest. At such times many people died of starvation.

Making meals

Bread was made from rye, oats or barley. Bread was only rarely made from wheat. Oatcakes were heated in milk or water to make porridge.

Honey was used for sweetening and also used to make an alcoholic drink called mead. Hops were grown to make beer.

Although the Vikings reared animals, they did not eat meat every day. Porridge and vegetable soups were the normal meals. Fish, eggs and meat were for special occasions.

Getting food in town

Most Vikings lived on farms in the country and very few in towns. Farming was extremely hard work and people often had little left over to sell.

This is why towns never grew to be large. There was simply not enough surplus (left-over) food to sell to the towns.

Who knows...

how much Vikings enjoyed their food?

Viking food was basic. This is a modern recipe based on what the Vikings may have eaten. Try it!

Viking porridge

▶ 15 cups of water.
▶ Two cups of chopped wheat kernels soaked overnight. Two cups of barley. Half a cup of coarse-ground wholewheat flour and half a cup of crushed nuts.
▶ 3 to 4 tablespoons of honey.
▶ Add the wheat and barley to the water and heat in a pot. As the porridge thickens, add the honey and nuts. It takes about half an hour to cook.

Weblink: www.CurriculumVisions.com

Longship

The Vikings could not have travelled the rough North Sea and Atlantic Ocean without a sturdy craft.

If you are going to travel across the open sea you must have a sturdy boat that will carry you in rough weather. Vikings built their boats in a number of sizes. They used most of them for carrying goods. However, they also made warships, and it is for these that they are most famous. The warships are what we know as **LONGSHIPS**.

▼ ① **A Viking longship. The ship's keel, or backbone, was made from a single piece of wood. To this were added the curved ends and the 'ribs' of the frame.**

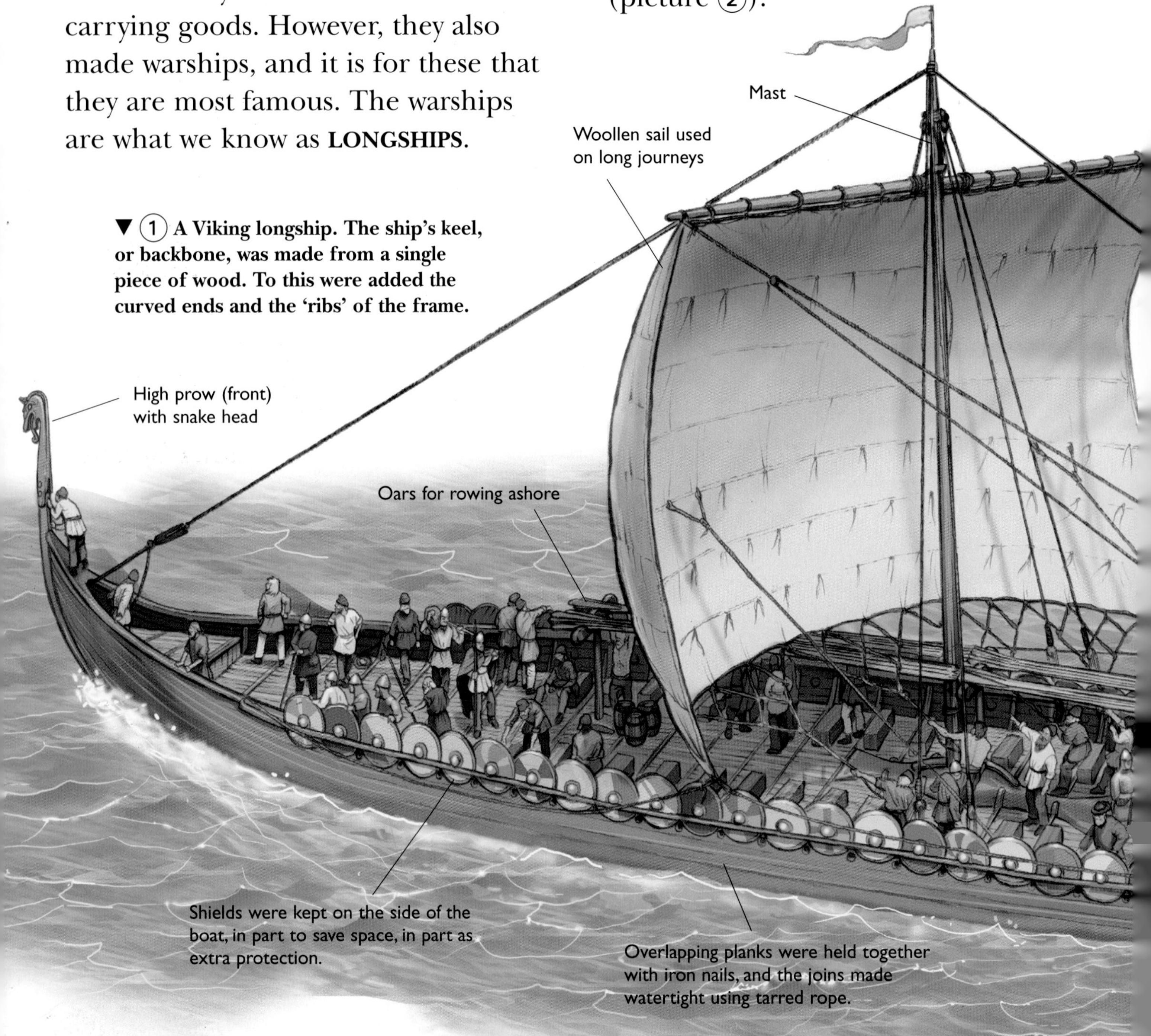

How the longship developed

Longships were developed over many centuries. The first boats made were dug out of solid logs (picture ②).

Mast

Woollen sail used on long journeys

High prow (front) with snake head

Oars for rowing ashore

Shields were kept on the side of the boat, in part to save space, in part as extra protection.

Overlapping planks were held together with iron nails, and the joins made watertight using tarred rope.

These dugouts were small and heavy.

Eventually, they built the longship, a sleek boat powered by oars and square sails (picture ①). It is a type of boat known as a **GALLEY**.

Boats had to be made of a hard wood, like oak, because a soft wood like pine would soak up water, rot and be eaten away by worms too quickly.

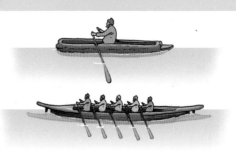

How longships were used

Longships were not large, about the size of a modern yacht – 15 to 25 metres long. They travelled at about 15 kilometres an hour.

The oarsmen sat on long benches, under which may have been a box containing their belongings. Shields were fastened on special racks along the sides. Placed like this they doubled up as protection from the weather and from enemy arrows.

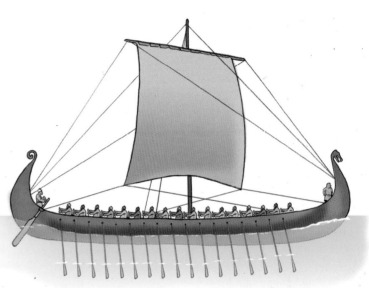

▲ ② Over the centuries, Viking boats evolved from small dugouts to the awesome longships.

Any booty or goods for trade had to be placed in the middle of the boat, where it could be protected from the weather by tent-like covers.

Sails were used for long journeys because rowing for days on end would have been too tiring. The oars were used for rowing up a river or for landing on a beach.

The longship was nearly flat-bottomed, which meant it was easy to use in shallow rivers and easy to beach. This is what made it so easy for Vikings to make sudden raids.

Rudder (tiller) for steering

The Vikings raid Britain

For centuries the Vikings had traded across Europe, but then they began to turn to piracy. The British Isles were easy targets.

▼ ① A Viking raid on the English coast. People were often captured rather than killed and became slaves.

Viking lands were poor and times could be very harsh. Often people were close to starvation.

Each CLAN fought battles with its neighbours for land, goods and captives – who were made into slaves.

As a result, Vikings became used to fighting. They began to think that the best way to get wealthier was to take what they wanted from others by violence.

These changes turned the Vikings into PIRATES. Raiding and piracy were very common at this time, but the Vikings were especially feared because of their swift boats and the violence of their attacks – and above all because they were successful.

The sea journey

The Vikings did not have compasses or maps to help them get to the British Isles. As a result, the chances

What the *Anglo-Saxon Chronicle* says about Vikings

The *Anglo-Saxon Chronicle* is a kind of diary of events written by the English (who at this time were called the Anglo-Saxons).

This is what the *Chronicle* has to say about the first ever raid on the British Isles. It clearly caught the Anglo-Saxons completely by surprise.

AD 793   *This year there were dreadful warnings over Northumbria, terrifying the people: these were immense sheets of light rushing through the air, and whirlwinds, and fiery dragons flying across the sky.*
These tremendous tokens were soon followed by a great famine; and not long after, in January, the heathen men [Vikings] made havoc in the church of God in Holy-island, by plunder and slaughter.

Sometimes the English were able to put up a fight, as happened in 794.

AD 794   *The heathen [Viking] armies spread devastation among the Northumbrians and plundered the monastery at the mouth of the Wear. There, however, some of their leaders were slain; and some of their ships also were shattered to pieces by the violence of the weather; many of the crew were drowned; and some, who escaped alive to the shore, were soon dispatched [killed] at the mouth of the river.*

of sailing off course were high. Some Viking ships never reached land and the sailors starved, lost in the open ocean. To give themselves a better chance of survival, they stored dried, salted or smoked fish on board, together with meat and water.

The small boats could also easily be damaged by great storms. Even after winning booty, many Vikings did not get back alive to Scandinavia, but drowned at sea.

The raids

Raids may have been made by a single ship or a group of ships (picture ①). Between 30 and 150 men might charge ashore to get what booty and captives they could find.

They didn't raid all of the time, and months might go by before another raid came. It was this uncertainty that made people in the British Isles afraid of the Vikings.

The raid

In our saga of the brave Bjorn, our hero is now a chieftain and makes raids on the shores of Britain.

It had been many days since Bjorn had last seen land. He was now a chieftain in his own right, and he had a band of trusty warriors with him.

Bjorn looked down the length of the longship that was under his command. Everyone was in high spirits. The ship was full of young men like himself, all eager to show off in front of their friends and to do daring deeds.

Everyone was relaxing. There was a good wind and the sail was carrying them along to their target – Britain. The oars were all stashed and the centre of the boat was still empty. 'Not for long,' thought Bjorn. 'There is plenty of room for gold and silver, a good load of beer and food, and even for some slaves.'

Bjorn expected no trouble when he got to Britain. He had been well trained in hit-and-run tactics, and in any case he was going to hit a soft target – a **MONASTERY**. 'Lots of booty and no one to protect it,' he said to himself. 'Golden goblets and other precious things that can all be taken with ease. The hardest work will be ripping the jewels off the covers of the books they call Bibles. Yes, it was going to be all too easy. Well, if they will be that careless with their valuables, they deserve to have them taken.'

Bjorn looked right and left to where other longships were keeping pace. Together they would make a fine attacking force.

There had been gulls flying overhead for some hours now – a sure sign that land was close. Then, suddenly there was a shout and someone pointed. There on the grey, sunless horizon, was a darker band of colour. There was no doubt about it – it was land.

The order was given, the sail furled, and oars put into the water. Now everyone got tense. Oars cut through the waves as they made their final approach to the shore. The dragon's head on the prow of the boat was a symbol of the warrior spirit of the men inside the boat. And so far there was no sign of defence, just people scurrying away so they would not be captured and taken as slaves.

'Yes,' thought Bjorn, 'This will be all too easy!'

(Note: this is a modern story; Viking sagas are too long to fit on this page. This is a story written to help you look at the raid in two different ways: from the point of view of those being invaded and from the point of view of the invaders.)

The Vikings invade

At first the Vikings just made hit-and-run raids. Gradually, they realised that they could gain new lands for their people, too.

Things were not going well for many Vikings at home. There were too many people wanting the same land. To some people, therefore, it seemed easier to find a new land to settle in. Many chose parts of the British Isles, while others chose what is now north-western France (Normandy) (picture ①). They **INVADED** these lands, brought over their families and set up new villages in the hope of better times.

Where the Vikings settled

The Danish Vikings invaded eastern England. They first stayed near London, fighting their way north to towns like York, which they renamed Jorvik.

To win land they had to fight big battles. Danes came across in their thousands to take part in the wars, led by fierce-looking noblemen, or jarls (picture ②).

The Norwegian Vikings sailed to the Shetlands, then the Orkneys and then the Western Isles of Scotland before moving on to Ireland.

▼ ① The routes the Norwegians and Danes took in raiding the British Isles.

▶ ② Viking noblemen wore iron helmets like this one.

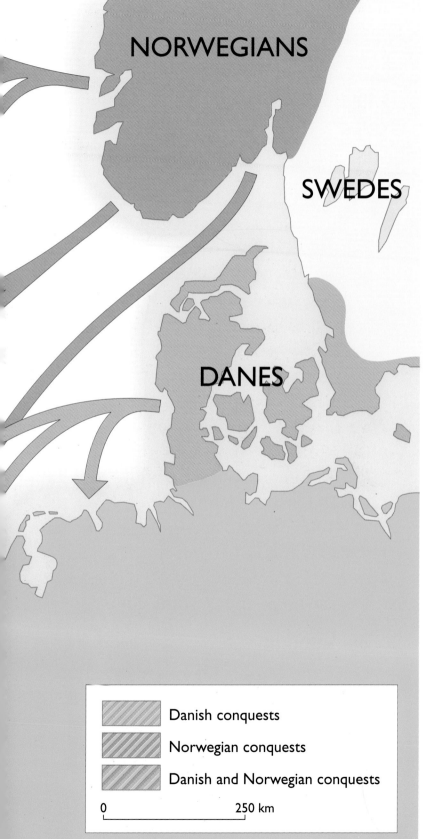

NORWEGIANS

SWEDES

DANES

Danish conquests

Norwegian conquests

Danish and Norwegian conquests

0   250 km

The Vikings completely overwhelmed the people of the Scottish islands, but they met their match in Ireland where there were already powerful kings. As a result, the Vikings invaded only the Irish coast, founding places like Dublin (Dyfflin).

Eventually, the Vikings were driven out of Ireland by the Irish kings. The Vikings then went over to the north-west coast of England (Cumbria) and to northern Wales (Anglesey is probably a Viking name).

The Danes also met their match in England. The Anglo-Saxons forced the invaders back eastward.

35

The Vikings in England

The Danish Vikings held part of England for centuries. The land they controlled was known as the Danelaw.

The first time anyone in England saw the Vikings as raiders was in 793 when they raided the Christian MONASTERY at Lindisfarne (Holy Island) in north-east England.

These were Danish Vikings. They burned the monastery, stole its treasures and killed many people.

Hit-and-run raids of this kind happened without warning for half a century. Then the Danes decided to invade and stay.

So many Danish Viking families came over to eastern England in 865 that it was called the year of the Great Invasion. The Danish king was called KING GUTHRUM. He knew that the only way to take control was to defeat the Anglo-Saxon kings of England. Over the next thirteen years the Danes slowly but surely won more ground.

The battle of Edington

One Anglo-Saxon leader in particular was to prove very hard to beat. This was KING ALFRED, ruler of the southern part of England called Wessex.

In the deep cold of mid-January 878 Guthrum's army attacked Alfred's army and forced it to retreat.

It was not until May 878 that Alfred felt his army was strong enough to fight back. Then he attacked, and this time it was Guthrum's army that had to retreat. It was all decided at a battle near Ethandun (now called Edington).

Both sides knew that neither was strong enough to completely crush the other. They were too evenly matched. Besides, more and more Vikings wanted to give up war and settle down. So the two sides agreed to divide the country between them.

Alfred's people kept the south-west, and Guthrum's people kept the north-east. The area where the Danes ruled came to be known as the DANELAW (picture ①).

Guthrum also agreed to stop being a pagan and to become a Christian. As a result, he changed his name to Ethalstan, meaning 'royal stone'.

Blending in

Once the Danish Vikings had begun to settle, they became 'English' and, as the generations passed, it became hard to tell the Viking people from anyone else. Only the names of the places they founded showed where they had originally come from.

But struggles over who should rule continued. One of the last rulers of all England just before the arrival of the Normans (who were also descended from Vikings) was King Canute, who was king of Denmark and England.

The *Anglo-Saxon Chronicle*

This is what the *Anglo-Saxon Chronicle* had to say about the way the Danes invaded.

AD 832   *This year heathen [Viking] men overran the Isle of Sheppey.*

AD 833   *This year fought King Egbert with thirty-five pirates at Charmouth, where a great slaughter was made, and the Danes remained masters of the field.*

AD 837   *This year Alderman Wulfherd fought at Hamton with thirty-three pirates, and after great slaughter obtained the victory, but he died the same year. Alderman Ethelhelm also, with the men of Dorsetshire, fought with the Danish army in Portland-isle, and for a good while put them to flight; but in the end the Danes became masters of the field and slew the alderman.*

AD 851   *This year the heathens now for the first time remained over winter in the Isle of Thanet. The same year came three hundred and fifty ships into the mouth of the Thames; the crew of which went upon land, and stormed Canterbury and London. [The West Saxon army] fought with them at Oakley and made the greatest slaughter of the heathen army that we have ever heard reported to this present day.*

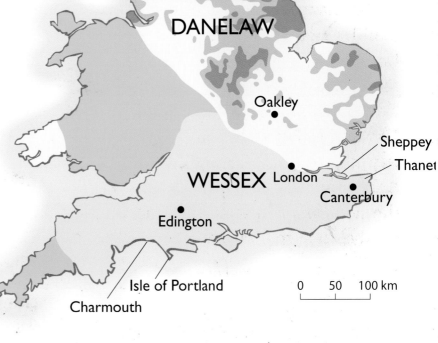

Placename endings of Scandinavian origin

Danelaw { Many / Few / None }

▲ ① The Danelaw area can be picked out from the rest of England by its place name endings. Common Scandinavian words used in place names throughout the Danelaw are: -by, -thorp, -trop, -thorpe, -toft, -thwaite, -holm, and -ness (for example Whitby, Scunthorpe).

When the Vikings conquered a place, they 'Vikingised' the name. For example, they changed Eoforwic to Jorvik, which was easier for Vikings to say. (After Viking times this name was shortened again to simply 'York'.)

The Vikings in Scotland

Scotland is the closest part of Britain to the Norwegian coast. Norwegian Vikings settled in the Northern Isles and remained there for 400 years.

The northern part of Britain was raided and then invaded by Norwegian Vikings. Like the Danish Vikings in England, the Norwegian Vikings were looking for a new homeland.

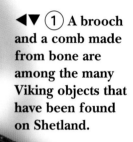

◀▼ ① A brooch and a comb made from bone are among the many Viking objects that have been found on Shetland.

There is little record of Vikings on the Scottish mainland. The Vikings mainly settled on the Northern Isles, including Shetland and Orkney. These were only sparsely populated, and their people could put up little defence. The Vikings quickly took over control and stamped their way of life on the islands.

The Vikings ruled these isles for centuries after the defeat of the Vikings of mainland Britain.

How they lived

There is no evidence of battles or of the slaughter of the island peoples. It seems that the pagan Vikings simply began to live alongside the Christian islanders. To begin with, each probably kept their own way of life. But as time went by, the communities merged under the rule of the Vikings.

A long period of control

The long period in which Shetland and Orkney were part of the Viking lands has left its mark on the landscape, place names and heritage of the islands. Evidence of the Vikings has, in some places, survived (pictures ① and ②).

◀ ② A stone from Shetland showing a Viking longship.

A vital link

The Vikings did not think of the Northern Isles just as land to live on. In the Viking world, the Northern Isles were an important base for travel between the British Isles and Norway. This is why they were settled for so long and why, at the end of the 9th century, the Northern Isles were made part of the kingdom of Norway.

From this time the islands were ruled on behalf of the Norwegian Viking king by a jarl. Sigurd the Mighty was the first jarl to rule Orkney. Shetland and Orkney finally became part of Scotland in 1472.

The land the Vikings once used has been as pastureland ever since. As a result, many early Viking houses have not been disturbed and their remains can still be seen (picture ③).

▼ ③ The remains of a Viking LONGHOUSE on the island of Unst, Shetland. The longhouse still shows remains of stone walls built over a thousand years ago. The wooden poles that made up the longhouse frame and the turf roof that once covered it have long since gone.

Weblink: www.CurriculumVisions.com

The first to the New World

When Leif, a chieftain in Iceland, was banned from the island for misdeeds, he sailed west and became the first European to reach America – the NEW WORLD.

The Vikings became great explorers. They didn't think of the British Isles as the end of the world. They had been island-hopping in the North Sea for centuries, and in this way they reached the Faeroe Islands and Iceland as well as all of the Scottish islands. They had also sailed around the coast of Spain and travelled the length of the Mediterranean Sea. (See the map on page 7.)

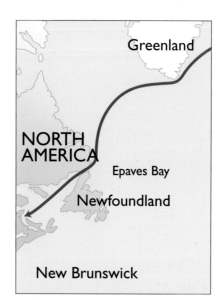

Epaves bay is on the northern tip of Newfoundland. (See page 7 for a complete version of this map.)

▶ ① There are remains of a Viking settlement on the northern tip of Newfoundland (see small map above), though we do not know whether this was Vinland. The map on the right shows what the settlement looked like. Here the Vikings had homes, workshops, a furnace and a place to work metal.

They used the sea to help defend their settlement and completed its defence by building a wooden fence in a semicircle. As a result, the plan of the Vinland settlement is D-shaped.

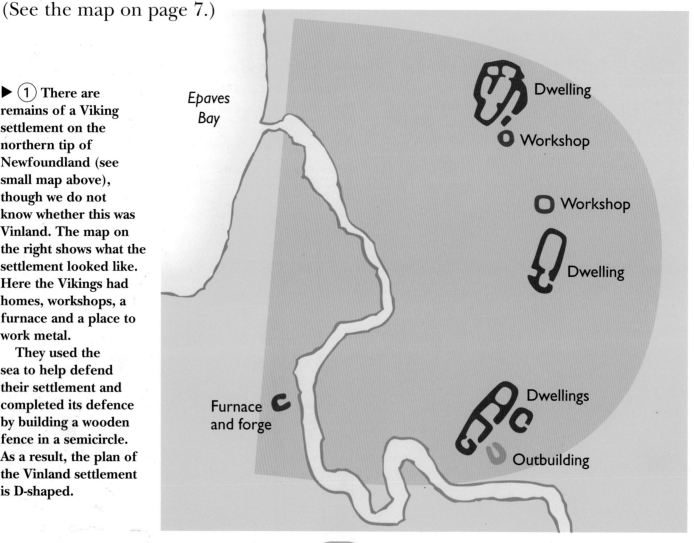

To the New World

Although they travelled around Europe, nobody knew what lay to the west of Greenland. Many people at this time thought that the world was flat and that if you sailed west you would fall off the edge of the Earth.

LEIF ERICSSON (known as Leif the Lucky) was the son of Eric the Red, a famous Viking who discovered Greenland. About one thousand one hundred years ago, in AD 1000, he led a small expedition that sailed west from Greenland. He reached a low, wooded coast at a place which may have been Newfoundland or New Brunswick (picture ① and inset).

Here the Viking explorers built some houses using stones, soil and grass (pictures ① and ②), but they only stayed a few months.

LEGEND tells of how they found juicy berries (probably cranberries), which they thought could be used to make wine. As a result, they called the newly discovered land Vinland.

For the next few years more people went to Vinland. By 1010, however, the Viking expeditions finished and from then on no one from Europe visited any part of North America until Christopher Columbus's famous voyage in 1492.

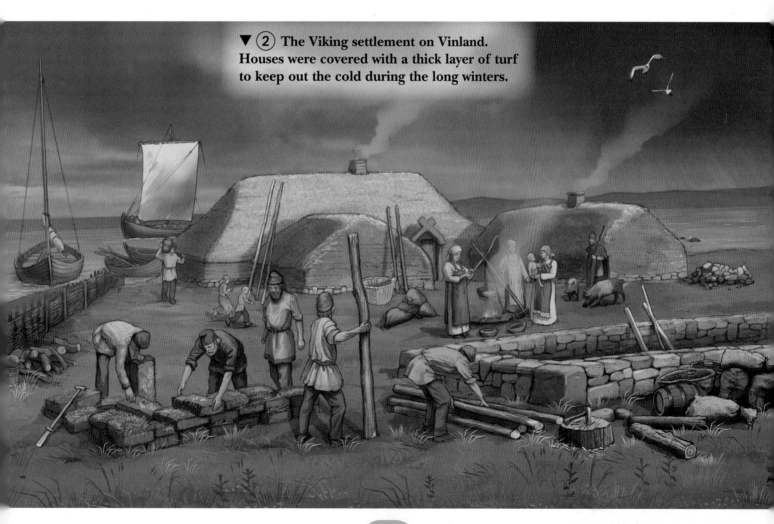

▼ ② The Viking settlement on Vinland. Houses were covered with a thick layer of turf to keep out the cold during the long winters.

The end of Viking times

As the Vikings were converted to Christianity they began to mix with the Anglo-Saxons and become simply British.

The Viking Age in England lasted from about 793 to 25 September 1066, when an invading Viking army was defeated by the Anglo-Saxon king of England Harold in a battle near York.

What happened to Vikings in England?

By then, the people who were descended from the original Viking invaders had been in the country so long that they thought of themselves as just as English as the Anglo-Saxons. They even helped to fight off the Vikings from Norway. It was all very different to when the first Vikings landed.

So, in many ways, the Viking Age was already at an end when the final battle was fought.

What happened in Scotland?

In Scotland, the Viking Age did not end at the same time as in England. For example, the people of the Northern Isles continued to be ruled by a Norwegian king. It was only in the 15th century, when King Christian of Norway wanted to marry his daughter to King James III of Scotland, that the Northern Isles were finally handed over to Scotland and 'Viking' influence ended.

What is left of the Vikings in Britain?

Today some people still have names that were once Viking (Thora, for example). Others carry Viking genes. This can be shown by testing the DNA in blood to see if it matches that typical of modern Scandinavians. So from this point of view Viking times never ended and there are still Vikings amongst us today!

▶ **Viking raids produced great hoards of treasure. This is part of a hoard of 8,500 silver objects found at Cuerdale, Lancashire. You can see coins, brooches, chains, rings and much more. The hoard weighs 40 kilograms! It was probably buried for safe keeping when Vikings were expelled from Ireland in 902. They never came back to collect it.**

▼ **Part of a carved stone (possibly a grave cover) found on Lindisfarne (Holy Island). It shows Viking warriors going into battle.**

A Viking timeline

AD

700 Vikings begin to trade around the coasts of Europe.

793 Norwegian Vikings begin to raid the coasts of the British Isles, beginning with the Northumberland monastery of Lindisfarne (Holy Island).

795 The Norwegian Vikings attack Iona in Scotland and Rechru in Northern Ireland.

800–830 The Vikings almost stop their raids.

830 Raiding begins again, this time on a bigger scale and by both Danish and Norwegian Vikings.

850 Danish Vikings spend the winter in Britain for the first time.

865 The Danes bring over a 'Great Army' to invade England.

866 The Danes capture York (Jorvik) from the Anglo-Saxons.

867 The Danes set out to capture more of England.

870 Iceland is discovered by Norwegian Vikings. By 930 ten thousand Vikings will have made it their home.

871 The Great Army of the Danes attacks the West Saxon kingdom of Wessex and defeats the army of King Alfred. Wessex pays off the Vikings in gold. (Secretly Alfred is buying time to assemble a new army.)

This protection money is called **DANEGELD**. The Danes take the money but still continue to advance.

871–878 King Alfred on the run. According to legend, during this time he takes refuge in a house and he allows some cakes to burn.

878 King Alfred assembles a new army and wins the battle against the Danes at Edington (Wiltshire). The Saxons and the Danes agreed to divide England between them. The land held by the Danes is called the Danelaw.

886 Alfred begins to win back some of the Danelaw by capturing London from the Danes.

937 King Athelstan defeats Vikings and Picts (Scots) in the Battle of Brunanburh and becomes "King of all Britain".

980 The Danes raid England again but do not stay.

991 Danish Vikings win important battles in Essex and are paid Danegeld by King Aethelred.

994 Danes under Sweyn and Norwegians under Trygvesson attack London and destroy London Bridge. They are bought off with more Danegeld.

1001 Norwegian Leif the Lucky is the first European to reach North America.

1003–
1013 Danes under Sweyn invade England. They are bought off several times, but simply use the money to buy more weapons and pay more troops.

1013 Sweyn lands in England and forces the Anglo-Saxon King Ethelred II into exile. Sweyn becomes king of Denmark and England.

1014 Sweyn dies, and the Anglo-Saxons offer the throne back to Ethelred.

1016 Sweyn's son Canute invades England. Canute becomes king of England and a powerful European ruler.

1035 Canute dies and his unpopular sons become king, first Harold, then Hardecanute.

1042 Viking reign in England ends when Hardecanute dies and the throne is offered back to the Anglo-Saxon kings.

1066 Harald Hadrade, Norwegian Viking king, tries to take the throne from Anglo-Saxon Harold, but is defeated.

1066 William of Normandy (who is also descended from Danish Vikings) invades England and becomes William the Conqueror.

2000 Most of us still have some Viking genes in us, but more if we come from the Scottish islands or from Cumbria in north-west England where Viking influence lasted the longest.

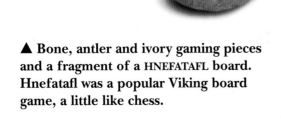

▲ Bone, antler and ivory gaming pieces and a fragment of a HNEFATAFL board. Hnefatafl was a popular Viking board game, a little like chess.

Words, names and places

AESIR A group of Viking gods. The Aesir included Odin, Thor, Frigg and Loki. The Vikings believed that Aesir lived in a world called Asgard. They called the world we live in Midgard, or 'Middle Earth'.

ALFRED, KING The most famous of the Anglo-Saxon kings who ruled parts of England at the time of the Viking invasions. He is famous for halting this invasion and is known as Alfred the Great.

ANGLO-SAXONS The inhabitants of England at the time of the Viking raids. The Anglo-Saxons had themselves invaded the country in the 5th century AD.

ARCHAEOLOGIST Someone who studies the remains of past cultures and peoples.

BALLAST Something heavy used to weigh down a boat in order to improve its stability and control.

BONDI A Viking farmer who also did duty as a warrior. He had given an oath of allegiance or had blood ties with a more powerful chieftain.

BOOTY Goods captured during a raid or war.

BREWERY A place where mead or beer is made (brewed).

CHAIN MAIL A cloth made of loops of iron. It was designed to protect the body from sword and spear blows.

CHIEFTAIN The leader of a tribe or clan.

CLAN A group of families closely related to one another and ruled by a chieftain.

DANEGELD (Dane = 'Danes'; geld = 'money'). A tax which was first raised from landowners between England in 991 and 1014 in order to buy off Danish Vikings from further attack.

DANELAW The area of England ruled by the Danes.

DYE A substance that can be used to colour cloth.

ERICSSON, LEIF The leader of the band of Vikings who were the first Europeans to settle in North America.

FJORD A long, narrow, rock-bound inlet from the sea; Norway has many fjords.

FLAX A fibrous plant that can be crushed and the fibres teased out and made into the textile called linen.

FORGE A workshop where metal is heated in a furnace and worked into objects such as tools or weapons.

FREY The name of the Viking god of life and justice.

FUTHARK The name of the Viking alphabet written in runes.

GALLEY An ancient ocean-going ship that used oars. Galleys usually also had sails. The Viking longship was a kind of galley.

GENERATION A group of people born about the same time. Your father and mother belong to the generation before you.

GREAT ARMY The army of several thousand warriors that the Danish Vikings organised to conquer England.

GUTHRUM, KING The king who led the Great Army of Danish Vikings when they invaded England.

HNEFATAFL A popular Viking board game, using bones, antler or ivory playing pieces.

INVADE To attack a country with an army.

JARL A Viking nobleman.

JORVIK The name of the most important town in Danish Viking England. Now called York. Although important, it was the size of a modern village.

KARL A Viking freeman, usually a farmer or a craftsman.

LEGEND A story about a famous person or event.

LONGHOUSE The large shared house that Vikings lived in.

LONGSHIP A fast galley ship with a woollen sail that the Vikings (and most other Europeans) used for seagoing voyages.

MIDDENS A layer of soil representing a place where waste from houses was tipped. Most of this material was waste food that has now decomposed, leaving only a dark staining to the soil. But middens also still contain items that are of great value to archaeologists such as food bones, pieces of stone and metal tools, pottery, and so on.

MONASTERY A settlement of Christian monks.

NEW WORLD A term used to describe America.

ODIN The main god of the Vikings. He was the god of war and wisdom.

PAGAN A person with religious beliefs different to the mainstream religions of the world. Pagans believe in a number of gods.

PIRATE A person who attacks and robs places and ships, usually using a ship for a quick getaway.

PRESERVE To keep for a long time.

QUERN A pair of flat stones used to grain corn by hand.

RAID To arrive quickly and take anything of value by force, then leave.

ROMANS A people who formed an empire centred on Rome more than 2,000 years ago. The Roman empire lasted for many hundreds of years and it was one of the greatest empires the world has ever known. The empire collapsed in the 5th century AD.

RUNE Any letter of the Viking alphabet.

SAGA A story made up to tell about famous people or events or simply to amuse, just as we would tell fairy stories. Sagas were an invention of the people of Iceland. Sagas were only written down two or three hundred years after the Viking raids. Sagas tell of the great days of Viking history and are a kind of folk memory of the past.

SCANDINAVIA The northern part of Europe including Denmark, Finland, Norway and Sweden.

SPINNING A way of twisting fibres to make a long thread. The first stage of making cloth.

THING An assembly of freemen in Scandinavia.

THOR One of the Viking gods. He was not very brainy but was good for fighting giants.

THRALL A Viking slave. Slaves would be soldiers, women and children captured in battle.

VALHALLA The name for the heaven in which warriors who died in battle lived with their god Odin. The Vikings thought of Valhalla as a beautiful palace with 540 doors and with a roof made of shields. The slain warriors spent their time feasting and fighting one another.

VIKING A Scandinavian warrior who lived at the times of the raids and invasions of the British Isles.

WARRIOR A fighting man who was paid by the amount of treasure he was able to get from the people he attacked.

WATTLE AND DAUB A framework of woven rods and twigs covered with clay; used by the Vikings to make buildings.

WEAVING/WOVE A way of making a cloth using thread.

Weblink: www.CurriculumVisions.com

Index